33 MASS LESSONS ᴀɴᴅ ACTIVITIES FOR CHILDREN

Patricia Mathson

TWENTY-THIRD PUBLICATIONS

twentythirdpublications.com

TWENTY-THIRD PUBLICATIONS
One Montauk Avenue, Suite 200
New London, CT 06320
(860) 437-3012 or (800) 321-0411
www.twentythirdpublications.com

Cover image: ©Shutterstock.com

ISBN: 978-1-62785-380-4
Library of Congress Control Number: 2018943225
Printed in the U.S.A.

 A division of Bayard, Inc.

CONTENTS

LITURGY OF THE EUCHARIST

CONCLUDING RITES

INTRODUCTION

This book is filled with ideas for connecting Sunday Mass to children's lives. As we explore the Mass with children, we invite them to experience God's presence and love. The Mass gives us a glimpse at how much God loves us. The celebration of the Mass should be at the center of our lives as disciples of Jesus Christ. We must also live the Mass in our lives during the week.

Celebrating Sunday Mass is something we joyfully do together as the people of God. We celebrate God's unending love for each of us and all of us. We want children to understand how they are part of a community of God's people that supports and loves them. We walk our faith journey together. The Mass reminds us of who God is and who we are as the people of God. We remember all that God has done for us. Participating in the Mass reminds us of what is important in life.

The Mass celebrates our relationship with God and with one another. Our actions show children who God is. When children know that God loves them, then they will be able to respond to God's love. It is important for children and all of us to understand that we participate in Sunday Mass not only to praise our God, but also to support other people by our presence and our prayers.

There are ideas and activities in this book for exploring each part of the Mass. A variety of activities are included that actively involve the children in learning. The ideas can be used in children's faith formation programs, Catholic schools, whole community catechesis, home school programs, family ministry, First Communion preparation, parish celebrations, with groups of families, and as part of a parish-wide study of the Mass.

The activities in this book are for children ages five to eleven but can be easily adapted for other age groups. The emphasis is on learning activities that speak to the way children learn. The ideas show children the importance of celebrating Sunday Mass together and living the Mass in our lives from Sunday to Sunday.

A strength of this book is the children's take-home idea. Sometimes, children have trouble grasping the central idea of a lesson, because it may include a lot of information or they may not understand what to do with the information presented to them. The children's take-home idea for each part of the Mass gives the children a simple reminder of what they learned and a practical suggestion for living it during the coming week.

There is a family page for each part of the Mass. This gives families some ideas of how to share the Mass with children and some activities they can do together at home. This supports parents as the primary teachers of their children in the ways of faith. There is also a prayer that families can pray together. The family activities show family members how to live the Mass in their lives.

In addition, there is a note to First Communion families at the bottom of each family page. This note is for families and extended families who are preparing children of any age to receive First Communion.

Through the Mass we celebrate who we are as God's people and all that God has done in our lives. We are renewed and strengthened by our time together and then go out to live as Jesus Christ showed us. As we walk with children though the Mass, we can help them explore the connection of Sunday Mass with their daily lives and the joy of being God's children.

→ *Why We Go to Mass*

Catechist notes

At Mass we are called to praise the God who created us, redeemed us, and lives in us. Assure children that God loves each one of us. We must help children connect Sunday Mass with how they live the other days of the week.

Sharing question

Why do we go to Sunday Mass?

Exploring the Mass

We come together at Sunday Mass to celebrate who God is and who we are as the people of God. The Mass is part of our identity as Catholics.

Reasons why Sunday Mass is important

- We lift up our hearts and our lives to the God who created us.
- We respond to God's unending love for each of us.
- We come as we are with our joys and sorrows and bring them to the Lord.
- Together we give thanks to God for all that God has done for us.
- We come to support one another with our prayers and our presence.
- Renewed, we go out after Mass to live what we believe.

At Mass we encounter God in the words of Scripture, in the Eucharist, and in one another. We participate as a community at Mass on Sundays because that is the day of the resurrection of Jesus Christ.

Learning activity

Make a heart poster

Show children how to make a heart poster to remember that God loves each of us. Write "God loves us with an unending love" on a sheet of poster board. Each child cuts a heart from red paper and puts their name on it. Then all children glue their hearts onto the poster.

When children know that God loves them, they will be able to respond to God in their own lives. Sunday Mass reminds children that all of us are on this faith journey together.

Children's take-home idea

Remember that God loves you with an unending love. Open your heart this week and look for God's presence in your life through the wonders of creation and the people who care about you. God will always be with you.

Praying together — *closing prayer.*

Awesome God,
on a Sunday you raised Jesus Christ to new life,
and the world was forever changed.
Guide us to come together at Sunday Mass
on the first day of each new week.
We remember that you are the hope
of our lives, of the world,
and of people everywhere.
Amen.

Why We Go to Mass

FAMILY IDEAS

The Mass is for all ages. We come together at Sunday Mass to celebrate who God is and who we are as the people of God. The Mass is part of our identity as Catholics. At Mass we encounter God in the word of Scripture, in the Eucharist, and in one another. Talk about why Sunday Mass is important to you and to the whole people of God.

▶ We respond to God who first loved us and gave us life. At Mass we give praise to our God for all God has done for us. Talk about the signs of God's love that we see in creation and in the people around us.

▶ We come to support one another with our prayers and our presence. We are all on this faith journey together. We thank God for all that God has done for us. We ask for the help we need for the week ahead. The Mass brings hope to our lives. Let's share hope with others too.

FAMILY PRAYER

Awesome God, we thank you for the gift of the Mass and your love for each of us. Help us to live in that love as a family and share your love with others. You are the hope of people everywhere. Amen.

Note to First Communion families

Encourage children preparing for First Communion to look for the good in life and in people. Teach them to have hope in God, hope in one another, and hope in the future. Hope is one of the most important gifts we can share with our children.

Gather Together

→ ## PART OF THE MASS: *Introductory Rites*

Catechist notes

When we come together for Sunday Mass, we bring all that has happened to us during the week. We bring our dreams, our disappointments, and ourselves to God. Children need to know that God loves each of us with an unending love.

Sharing question

Why does God care about what is going on in our lives?

Exploring the Mass

God created us and has loved us since before we were born. The Mass is a gift that celebrates our relationship with God and with one another. We bring our cares and concerns before the Lord. We join our prayers with our parish community at Mass. We gather together to give praise to our God. The first part of the Mass is called the Introductory Rites.

Parts of the Introductory Rites

- Opening song
- Sign of the Cross
- Penitential Act
- Lord, have mercy
- Glory to God (omitted during Advent and Lent)
- Opening Prayer (Collect)

Learning activity

Join in an action prayer

We come together as a community in the Introductory Rites at Mass to give praise to God.

We want children to know the joy of being God's children and of having a relationship with God.

Children can pray to God with an action prayer. This activity does not depend on good reading skills. Children echo the words and actions of the catechist line after line.

God of all people,	*arms overhead*
we give you glory and praise	*nod head*
for your unending love for us.	*hands on heart*
May we listen to your voice	*hands behind ears*
speaking in our hearts	*hands over heart*
at Mass and in our lives.	*nod head*
Guide us to follow you	*walk in place*
and share your love	*hands on heart*
with other people each day.	*arms outstretched*
Amen.	*praying hands*

Children's take-home idea

Share your hopes and concern this week with God, who is always with you. Remember that God has loved you since before you were born. Pray in your own words and know that God hears your prayers.

Praying together

God of all people,
we give you praise and glory
for creating us and calling us to life.
When we gather together at Mass,
help us to show love for you and others.
Guide us to live as a community of your people
after we leave Mass also. Amen.

PART OF THE MASS:
Introductory Rites

FAMILY IDEAS

At Mass we join our prayers together in praise of our God. We celebrate God's unending love for us. We bring our cares and concerns before the Lord. We support one another at Sunday Mass with our presence and our prayers.

▶ We want children to know the joy of being God's children. Encourage children to delight in God's love and God's creation. Point out signs of God's love in the world: people who care about us, sunshine to give light to our days, and music to speak to our hearts.

▶ Encourage children's participation in Sunday Mass by how you talk. Stress that we *get to* go to Mass, rather than we *have to* go to Mass. Make participating in Mass a priority when you plan your family's schedule.

FAMILY PRAYER

God of all people, we know that you created us and call us to life with you. When we gather at Mass, help us to praise you together. May we lift up our hearts and our voices to you. Help our family praise you by our words and actions each day. Amen.

Note to First Communion families

As we come together at Mass, ask God's help to prepare your child to receive First Communion. Involve extended family by asking them to pray for your child and share their faith stories. Getting ready for First Communion enriches all of us as we remember the importance of the sacrament of the Eucharist in our own lives.

People of God

→ PART OF THE MASS: *Opening Song*

Catechist notes

The opening song at Mass unites us. Together we give praise and glory to God. Music touches our hearts and fills us with joy. Music is a part of Mass all over the world as people raise their hearts and voices to God. We begin and end our celebration of the Mass together in song.

Sharing question

Why do we begin Mass by singing a song together?

Exploring the Mass

The opening song unites us as the people of God. We joyfully come together as we get ready to begin our celebration of the Mass. We praise our God together. As we sing, the entrance procession begins, led by an altar server carrying the cross. The Book of the Gospels is also brought forward. The celebrant of the Mass comes in at the end of the procession.

Music is part of who we are as God's people. Music is a God-given gift. We are all called to join together by lifting our hearts and our voices in song as we celebrate Sunday Mass. Guide the children to understand that music helps us express our joy at being God's creation.

Learning activity

Encourage children to sing

Encourage children to sing at Mass by helping them become familiar with some of the music. Reassure children that if they don't know all the words, they can sing just the refrain to give praise to God.

Another idea is to pick one gathering song and discuss the words and message with the children. One song often sung as an opening song is "All Are Welcome" by Marty Haugen. Talk about the words in each verse. Sing the song with the children, and add simple gestures if you choose.

Children's take-home idea

Give praise to God this week with music. Sing a song of praise to God or listen to a Christian song on your iPad or other device. God has given us the gift of music that speaks to our hearts. Listen for the message of the song.

Praying together

Loving God,
we praise you as the Creator of all people,
made in your image and likeness.
Teach us to love one another
as you love each one of us.
May our words, our actions, and our songs
at Mass give glory to you now and forever.
Amen.

PART OF THE MASS:
Opening Song

FAMILY IDEAS

The opening song at Mass unites us as the people of God. Through the God-given gift of music, we give praise and glory to God. Songs help us express what we believe. Music touches our hearts and fills us with joy as we lift up our voices to God.

▶ Encourage your child to sing with the parish community at Mass. It is fine to sing only the refrain of a song. For children who enjoy singing, check on the age requirement for the children's choir.

▶ Invite children to have joy in being children of God. In the car, play a music CD with catchy tunes about God's love, and sing along. Download a song you sing at Mass to your phone and listen to it when you are together. Talk about what it means to you all.

FAMILY PRAYER

Loving God, we gather together at Mass to give you praise for your unending love for us. Teach our family to love others as you love each of us. May our words, our actions, and our songs at Mass give glory to you now and forever. Amen.

Note to First Communion families

Encourage your child to participate fully in the Mass by singing the songs and saying the prayers. We join our voices with others at Mass as the people of God. This helps us to celebrate the Eucharist in our minds and hearts.

Believe in Jesus

➜ PART OF THE MASS: *Sign of the Cross*

Catechist notes

Before he died, Jesus told his apostles to baptize "in the name of the Father, and of the Son, and of the Holy Spirit" (Matthew 28:19). We begin our celebration of the Mass with the Sign of the Cross as a sign of faith in God. We remember all that God has done for us.

Sharing question

Why do we begin Mass with the Sign of the Cross?

Exploring the Mass

We start each Mass with the Sign of the Cross as a reminder of our baptism and our faith in Jesus Christ as the Savior of the world. At baptism we were signed with the cross by our parents and godparents. At Mass we do it on our own.

The cross reminds us of how much God loves us. It is a sign and a promise that we are to live as disciples of Jesus Christ. We are people created by the Father, redeemed by the Son, and guided by the Holy Spirit. The Sign of the Cross reminds us that we are not alone, because God is always with us.

Learning activity

Put together sun catcher crosses

Encourage children to make individual stained-glass crosses as a reminder of the Sign of the Cross. Each child cuts out a large paper cross. Then they cut out the middle of the cross leaving just a ½-inch-wide outline. Children place their crosses on clear, self-adhesive shelf covering. They overlap squares of colored tissue paper inside the cross outline.

Help each child carefully cover his or her cross with another sticky sheet and then cut around the outside. This makes beautiful crosses to put in a window and let the sun shine through. The colorful crosses are a visual reminder that we called to follow Jesus in our lives.

Children's take-home idea

The Sign of the Cross is an act of faith in our God. It reminds us and others that we are disciples of Jesus Christ. Every time you make the Sign of the Cross this week, remember how much God loves you.

Praying together

Almighty God,
we have faith in you and thank you
for all that you have done for us.
Helps us to live our faith
by what we say and do each day.
We pray in the name of the Father
who created us, the Son who redeemed us,
and the Holy Spirit who guides our lives.
Amen.

BELIEVE IN JESUS:
Sign of the Cross

FAMILY IDEAS

We begin our celebration of the Mass with the Sign of the Cross as a prayer of faith in our God. The Sign of the Cross is also as a reminder of our baptism. We belong to God's family. We are people created by the Father, redeemed by the Son, and guided by the Holy Spirit.

▶ Display a cross in your home as a daily reminder that we called to live as disciples of Jesus Christ. There are a wide variety of crosses available, from a simple wooden cross to a beautiful painted cross. You can also make your own cross with your children.

▶ Encourage your children to make the Sign of the Cross with holy water as they enter the church for Mass. Explain that this is a sign of what we believe. When we make the Sign of the Cross, we remember that God is always with us.

FAMILY PRAYER

Almighty God, we ask that you bless our family today in all that we do and wherever we go. We pray this in the name of the Father who created us, the Son who redeemed us, and the Holy Spirit who guides our lives. Amen.

Note to First Communion families

Think about getting your child a cross as a First Communion gift. It can be a cross for their bedroom, if they don't already have one, or even a cross necklace.

Ask Forgiveness

→ PART OF THE MASS: *Penitential Act*

Catechist notes

As a community of God's people, we ask God's forgiveness and we forgive others. We can be confident that God will always forgive us. (During the Easter season the rite of blessing with holy water may be used at the time of the Penitential Act.)

Sharing question

How can we do wrong by what we don't do?

Exploring the Mass

At Mass we pray the Penitential Act together. We ask God to forgive us for what we have done wrong and also for what we have failed to do right. When we do not make God a priority in our lives and when we could have made a difference in the life of someone else but did not step forward, we fail to be the people God created us to be.

We also ask our brothers and sisters to pray for us. We are a community of God's people and must support one another and forgive one another. God will never turn away from us. We encounter God's mercy and love at each Mass.

Learning activity

Draw peacemaker pictures

The Penitential Act reminds us that we are called to be people who live in peace. We are to forgive others as God forgives us. Talk with the children about living in peace with others.

Living in peace

▶ Ask forgiveness of others.
▶ Treat other people with dignity and respect.
▶ Stop making excuses when we do something wrong.
▶ Use words to bring healing, not hurt.
▶ Make friends with new people.
▶ Stand up for the rights of others.

Ask each child to draw a picture of themselves being a peacemaker. Then give children the opportunity to share their pictures with the group.

Children's take-home idea

God calls us to be peacemakers in the lives of others. Look for opportunities this week to live in peace. Make a choice to be who God created you to be. Use your words to bring peace and healing to the lives of others.

Praying together

God of forgiveness,
we ask your forgiveness for the times
we have hurt others by our words and actions.
Forgive us also for the times
when we have failed to do what is right.
Guide us to live in mercy and forgiveness
and to be peacemakers in our lives each day.
Amen.

ASK FORGIVENESS:
Penitential Act

FAMILY IDEAS

We pray the Penitential Act together at Mass. One form of it begins, "I confess to Almighty God and to you, my brothers and sisters..." What we do or fail to do affects other people. When we do not reach out a helping hand or we ignore injustices done to others, we are not living as God created us to live.

▸ Be sure your children understand that God will always forgive us when we ask. We don't have to earn forgiveness. God loves us with an unending love and will never turn away from us. God is a God of mercy and love. We can trust our God always.

▸ Talk with your children about living in peace. We are called to share God's forgiveness with others. We can be peacemakers by using our words and actions to bring healing and not hurt to others. Talk about how to do this together as a family.

FAMILY PRAYER

God of second chances, we know that you call us to live in peace in our family and in our world. We ask your forgiveness for the times in our lives when we have hurt other people by our words or actions. Guide us to live always with love for others in our lives and in our hearts. Amen.

Note to First Communion families

One way to get ready to celebrate First Communion is to forgive people in our lives who have hurt us. This does not mean that what they did was right, but grudges only hurt the people who hold them. Ask your child to think of ways to let go of anger, such as listening to music or talking to someone they trust.

God Is Merciful

➜ **PART OF THE MASS:** *Lord, Have Mercy*

Catechist notes

The "Lord, have mercy" prayer is also called the *Kyrie*. This prayer has been prayed for centuries as part of the Mass. It is a reminder that God is a God of mercy and forgiveness. We pray that God will have mercy on us.

Sharing question

How do we know that God will always forgive us?

Exploring the Mass

Jesus showed us by his words and actions that our God is a God of mercy. In the gospels we see time and again that Jesus forgave people for their sins. Even from the cross Jesus forgave others. Our merciful God will always forgive us.

At Mass the priest asks God to have mercy on us, and the assembly echoes the words. We can trust in God. God will be there when we face challenges or difficulties. God created us, loves us, and will never turn away from us. Sometimes we may turn away from God. Then God waits for us to turn back toward the light of God's love for us.

Learning activity

Make a "Lord, have mercy" poster

Share with children the story of the Pharisee and the tax collector in Luke 18:10–14. Explain that the people of Jesus' time would have been surprised that the tax collector was the one who was "right with God." Point out that the tax collector did not make excuses but asked God for mercy. We too can trust in God's mercy.

Making a "Lord, have mercy" poster can help personalize the prayer we say together at Mass. To make a group poster, write the words "Lord, have mercy" on a sheet of poster board. Each child cuts out an individual purple cross from construction paper. Provide patterns if needed. Then ask children to write their name on their individual cross with a black marker. They glue the crosses to the poster as a reminder to ask for God's mercy in their lives. Display the poster where the children can see it.

Children's take-home idea

Keep in mind that God is a God of mercy and compassion who loves us always. You can always trust God. God will never turn away from you. Share God's mercy with someone else this week.

Praying together

God of mercy.
we know that you are a God
of forgiveness and compassion
and that you will always forgive us.
May we show mercy to other people
as you always show mercy to us.
Amen.

GOD IS MERCIFUL:
Lord, Have Mercy

FAMILY IDEAS

The "Lord, have mercy" prayer has been prayed for centuries as part of the Mass. It is a reminder that God is a merciful God and a God of forgiveness. Even from the cross Jesus forgave others. Our merciful God will always forgive us.

▶ We are called to ask forgiveness of God and of one another. Teach your children to make up in some way for what they do wrong. A mumbled "sorry" is okay, but a child who called someone a name should also try to say something nice to the other child.

▶ Read Bible stories together about how our God is a merciful God. Jesus told people the story of the prodigal son (Luke 15:11–32). Talk about what this story shows us about who God is. God is like the forgiving Father who runs out to forgive us and welcome us home.

FAMILY PRAYER

God of mercy, we know that you love us and will never turn away from us. May we show mercy to other people as you show mercy to each of us. Guide us to be people of forgiveness in all things. Amen.

Note to First Communion families

As Eucharistic people, we are to live in mercy. We come together before God at Mass and ask for mercy. We are also to show mercy to others. Ask children to think of ways to do this, such as using words to heal, not hurt, others or helping a new child at school.

Give Praise to God

➜ **PART OF THE MASS: *Glory to God***

Catechist notes

We sing together and give glory and praise to God at this part of the Mass. This important prayer of praise honors our God who is Father, Son, and Holy Spirit. (The "Glory to God" prayer is not used during the seasons of Advent and Lent or at most weekday Masses.)

Sharing question

Where do the first words in the Glory to God prayer come from?

Exploring the Mass

At Mass we pray together: "Glory to God in the Highest." We echo the words of the angels to the shepherds when Jesus was born in Bethlehem (Luke 2:14). We lift up our hearts and our voices and give praise to our God, who created us, loves us, and is always with us. We are called to have a relationship with God.

Each Sunday is a time to celebrate anew all that God has done and continues to do in our lives. We give glory to God at Mass and then go out to give glory to God by what we say and do throughout the week.

Involve children in taking a close look at the words of the *Gloria* by giving out copies of this prayer. Ask each child to circle words that speak to their hearts, such as peace, thanks, praise, glory, mercy, and prayer. Talk about what these words mean to us and why they are important.

Learning activity

Make a mosaic craft

Encourage children to give glory to God not only at Mass but during the week too. Show them how to make a craft to display at home. Ask children to print the words "Glory to God in the Highest" on half sheets of card stock. Frame the words with 5 x 7-inch foam frames from a craft store or online catalog.

Provide several colors of self-stick foam. Help the children cut out small squares and then cut those diagonally to make triangles. Children peel off the backing and arrange the pieces on the frame to make a mosaic pattern.

Children's take-home idea

We give glory to God by the way we live our lives each day. This week give glory to God through your prayers, your words, and your actions. Think of at least one way you can do this during the week ahead.

Praying together

God of heaven and earth,
we give honor and praise to you.
Bless our words and our actions,
that we may give glory to you
in all that we do today and always.
Glory to God in the highest!
Amen.

GIVE PRAISE TO GOD:
Glory to God

FAMILY IDEAS

When we say together the "Glory to God" prayer together, we give praise to the God of all of us. We lift up our hearts and our lives at Mass to God, who created us, loves us, and is always with us. Each Sunday is a time to celebrate anew all that God has done and continues to do in our lives.

▶ Explain to your children that the first words of this prayer come from the words of the angels to the shepherds when Jesus was born in Bethlehem (Luke 2:14). Each Sunday at Mass we come together to praise God.

▶ Explore the idea that we are to continue giving glory to God during the week by what we say and do. Share ideas, such as thanking God for blessings, praying each day, showing respect to people of all cultures, making good choices, sharing the good news of Jesus Christ, and doing acts of kindness for others.

FAMILY PRAYER

God of heaven and earth, we give glory and praise to you and remember all you have done for us. Bless our words and actions at Mass and at home, so that our family may give glory to you each day. Glory to God in the highest. Amen.

Note to First Communion families

First Communion is an opportunity for families and the parish community to recall all that this sacrament means to us. We not only receive the Eucharist at Mass, but we are to live it in our lives after Mass. We are called to give glory to God each day by our words and actions.

Pray Together

→ **PART OF THE MASS:** *Opening Prayer*

Catechist notes

The opening prayer at Mass is called the Collect because it sums up and collects all the prayers of the people. The priest prays this prayer for us and with us. We love God and pray to God because God first loved us. God always hears our prayers.

Sharing question

Why is prayer so important?

Exploring the Mass

Through prayer, we talk to God and God speaks to us. Prayer is an important part of our relationship with God, who created us and loves us. Just like we talk to our friends and make time for them, so we should talk to God in prayer. The prayers of the Mass help us to express to God what is in our hearts.

Who we are and who God is in our lives are reflected in the prayers of the Mass. The opening prayer is different each Sunday. At the end of the opening prayer the presider says, "One God for ever and ever." We make the prayer our own when we respond "Amen."

Learning activity

Assemble prayer boxes

Explore with the children the idea that we are to pray in our lives beyond Sunday Mass. What we begin at Mass should be lived in our lives. Show children how to make individual prayer boxes to help them pray. These boxes can be adapted for all ages and abilities. Get school supply boxes that children label "Prayer Box" on top. Help children assemble or make items to be included.

Items for prayer boxes

- picture of God's creation
- heart as a sign of God's love
- holy card with the Lord's prayer
- words to a psalm of praise
- list of people to pray for
- pray always Bible verse
- cross to remember to follow Jesus

Children's take-home idea

Pray each day this week when you get up in the morning. Offer the day to the God who created you and loves you and wants only the best for you. Each day is an opportunity for us to begin anew.

Praying together

Bless our thoughts, Lord,
that we may give you praise.
Bless our words, Lord,
that we may proclaim your love.
Bless our actions, Lord,
that we may serve others.
Amen.

PRAY TO OUR GOD:
Opening Prayer

FAMILY IDEAS

The prayers of the Mass help us to express to God what is in our hearts. The opening prayer is different each Sunday. As the people of God we should pray not only at Sunday Mass, but also during the week. Encourage your children to be people of prayer.

▶ Encourage children to pray each morning. Offer the day to the God who created you and loves you and wants only the best for you. Each day is a gift and an opportunity to begin anew. Morning prayer gets each day off to a better start and gets us headed in the right direction.

▶ Have family prayer partners this week. Put each person's name on a paper heart in a bowl. Then each family member draws a name and prays for that person throughout the coming week. Prayer unites us not only with God, but with one another.

FAMILY PRAYER

Lord of all, we know that you are always with our family. Help us to turn to you in prayer each day and pray for the needs of other people in our world. Send your Holy Spirit to guide our hearts and our lives. Amen.

Note to First Communion families

Pray for the child in your family who is preparing for First Communion. You can add a short prayer after you say grace or bedtime prayers together. This helps children feel loved and special and teaches them to pray in all things.

Listen to God's Word

➡ ## Part of the Mass: *Liturgy of the Word*

Catechist notes

There are four Scripture readings during the Liturgy of the Word, which are all proclaimed from the ambo. This includes the first reading, psalm, second reading, and gospel. At weekday Masses, there is only one reading plus the psalm and gospel.

Sharing question

Why do we have readings from the Bible at Mass?

Exploring the Mass

The second part of the Mass is the Liturgy of the Word. God speaks to us and our lives through the words of Scripture. We learn how much God loves us and how we are to live as disciples of Jesus Christ. The word of God is handed on from generation to generation in the church through the Holy Spirit. We can also read and study the Bible beyond the Mass.

Parts of the Liturgy of the Word

First reading	Gospel
Psalm	Homily
Second reading	Creed
Alleluia	Prayers of the faithful

Learning activity

Do a Bible tour

Encourage children to learn more about God's word with a Bible tour. This gives them a hands-on look at the Bible. Each child needs a Bible to use. Explain that there are two main parts in the Bible. Ask them to turn to the first part. The Old Testament is the story of God and the people. This is our story too. The first book, Genesis, begins with the story of God creating the heavens and the earth. Other books tell how the people sometimes turned away from God, but God was always faithful to them.

Turn to the second part of the Bible. The New Testament is the story of Jesus Christ and the early church. In the New Testament there are four gospels—Matthew, Mark, Luke, and John—about the life and teachings of Jesus. After the gospels, the rest of the New Testament is about the people of the early church and how they shared the good news with others. We are called to do this too. The Bible is the story of God's unending love for us.

Children's take-home idea

God speaks to us through the words of Scripture. Listen carefully to the readings at Mass the next time you go. Look for one idea or one word that speaks to your heart and your life.

Praying together

God of the universe,
open our minds to your word
in Scripture so that we can learn about you.
Open our hearts to your love
so that we may share love with others.
Open our hands to serve others
in your holy name.
Amen.

PART OF THE MASS:
Liturgy of the Word

FAMILY IDEAS

The Liturgy of the Word at Mass begins with the first reading. God speaks to us through the words of Scripture. Four readings from the Bible are proclaimed at each Sunday Mass. In Scripture we learn how much our God loves us.

▶ Share Bible stories with your children from your own Bible, or download a Bible to your cell phone.
Good Bible stories to start with are Jesus and the children (Mark 10:13–16) and the good Samaritan (Luke 10:29–37).

▶ Encourage children to listen for one word in the readings or homily at Mass that speaks to them. After Mass, share as a family the word each person remembers and why it is important. This helps children focus on the message for their lives.

FAMILY PRAYER

God of the universe, open our minds to your word in Scripture so we can learn about you at Mass and at home. Open our hearts to your love so that we may love others in your name. Open our hands so that our family may serve others. Amen.

Note to First Communion families

A Bible makes a good First Communion gift for children. Depending on your child's reading ability, it can be a children's Bible or a colorful youth Bible. Other suitable gifts include a children's prayer book or books about saints for children. Suggest this type of meaningful gift to relatives too.

➥ PART OF THE MASS: *First Reading*

Catechist notes

We are people who have the written word of God as well as church teaching to guide us. The first reading at Mass is from the Old Testament except in the Easter season when we hear from the Acts of the Apostles.

Sharing question

Why is the first reading at Mass from the Old Testament?

Exploring the Mass

The Old Testament is the story of God and God's people, so it is our family story too. These Scriptures show us that God is always faithful to us. We sit and listen as the word of God is proclaimed from Scripture. The lector proclaims the readings at Mass from a book called the lectionary.

An example of a first reading is Jeremiah 29:11–14. It begins "I know the plans I have for you, says the LORD, to give you a future with hope." The prophet Jeremiah reminded people that with God we always have hope. One of the greatest gifts we can share with the next generation is hope in God and hope in the future.

Learning activity

Learn with a hope echo pantomime

It is important for children to understand that Scripture speaks to our lives today. An echo pantomime can help children learn that God brings hope. Say each line and do the actions, then the children echo, line by line.

Hope echo pantomime

For I know the plans I have for you,	*hands outstretched*
says the LORD.	*arms raised overhead*
Plans for a future of hope.	*nod head*
When you call me,	*hands by mouth*
when you go to pray to me,	*hands folded*
I will listen to you.	*hands behind ears*
When you look for me,	*look from side to side*
you will find me.	*nod head*
When you seek me	*walk in place*
with all your heart,	*hands on heart*
you will find me with you,	*hug self*
says the LORD.	*arms raised overhead*

Children's take-home idea

Look for the good in each day. We are called to have hope in God, hope in one another, and hope in the future. Live in hope and share that hope with someone else this week. In this way we live as God created us.

Praying together

God of hope,
we know that the story of your people
in Scripture is our story too.
Help us to listen to the readings
at Mass so we can learn your word.
Create in us hearts full of hope
so we may share hope with others.
Amen.

Part of the Mass:
First Reading

FAMILY IDEAS

We hear the first reading at Mass from the Old Testament. The Old Testament is the story of God and God's people, so it is our family story too. The stories of the Old Testament show us that God is always faithful to us. Hope is one of the most important ideas we can share with the next generation.

▶ It is important for us to show our children that there is good in the world. Point out to children examples of people who reach out to help one another in your community and world. In that way we begin to take the focus off the many negative things they see and hear in their lives.

▶ Share hope with your children. We are called to have hope in God, hope in one another, and hope in the future. This is how God created us to live. Talk about the future and the possibilities it brings.

FAMILY PRAYER

God of hope, we know that the story of your people in Scripture is our story too. Help us to listen to the readings at Mass so we can learn your word. Create in us hearts full of hope so that our family may share hope with others. Amen.

Note to First Communion families

Preparing to receive the Eucharist for the first time is an opportunity to help children recognize the God-given gifts they have that can be shared with others. They may have the gift of music, listening skills, compassion for the elderly, ability to do art, and more. Guide them to share these gifts with other people.

Celebrate Our God

→ PART OF THE MASS: *Responsorial Psalm*

Catechist notes

As a community of God's people, we join together to thank God for all God has done for us. The psalm is sung by the cantor, and we sing the response. The psalms have been prayed by God's people for thousands of years.

Sharing question

Why do we give praise to God?

Exploring the Mass

We were created to praise the God who loves us and made a wonderful world for us to share. Our God is the source of all blessings. As we sing out the psalm response together at Mass, we lift up our voices to praise our God together.

Examples of psalm verses

- Give thanks to God, bless God's name. (Psalm 100:4)
- Blessed be the name of the Lord. (Psalm 113:2)
- This is the day the Lord has made, let us rejoice and be glad. (Psalm 118:24)
- Praise the name of the Lord. (Psalm 135:1)
- Every day I will bless you and praise your name forever. (Psalm 145:2)

Explore the idea with the children that we honor God when we take care of the world God has given us to share. At Mass we give praise to God for all of creation, and then during the week we do the work of protecting our planet and the resources we have been given to share.

Learning activity

Design a psalm banner

Children can make individual psalm banners to celebrate God. Each child writes a psalm verse on paper. For younger children make copies of the words before the children gather. Children glue their psalm prayer to a sheet of colored card stock.

Then they use foam stickers of stars, animals, hearts, and flowers to decorate the outer edge of the banner. Children then punch holes in the two upper corners and use yarn to make a hanger. The beautiful psalm banner is displayed at home as a reminder to praise our God.

Children's take-home idea

Remember that God created you and loves you. Praise God this week with the words of a psalm. Use the psalm from your poster, a psalm from Mass, or another psalm that helps you lift up your heart to God.

Praying together

God of blessings,
we give you thanks for the world
you have created for love of us
and the people who share our faith journey.
May we give you praise in the words of the psalms,
as people have done for generations.
Amen.

PART OF THE MASS:
Responsorial Psalm

FAMILY IDEAS

People at Mass respond with the psalm response to praise our God. The psalms give us words to celebrate who God is in our lives. Through the psalms we join our prayers with people who are praying the psalms all over the world.

▶ Make psalm postcards. Print psalm verses such as "This is the day the Lord has made; let us rejoice and be glad." (Psalm 118:24) on colorful index cards. Add a sticker, such as a sun, flower, or heart. Give a postcard to each family member to place where they will see it and be reminded to praise God during the coming week.

▶ Explore the idea with the children that we honor God when we take care of the world God has given us to share. At Mass we give praise to God for all of creation, and then during the week we do the work of protecting our planet and the resources we have been given to share. Talk about ways to do this.

FAMILY PRAYER

God of blessings, we give you thanks for the world you have created for love of us and the people who share our faith journey. Renew our hearts and our lives so that our family may give praise to you at Mass and in all we do. Amen.

Note to First Communion families

Being a first Communion family is a time to give praise to God in our hearts and in our lives. Choose a beautiful psalm verse to print off a website such as Pinterest. Frame it and display in your home as a reminder to give thanks and praise to God.

We Are the Church

→ ## PART OF THE MASS: *Second Reading*

Catechist notes

After the resurrection of Jesus Christ, the disciples spread the good news far and wide. They knew that Jesus Christ came for all people. The words of the second reading at Mass guide our lives as disciples of Jesus Christ.

Sharing question

How can we share the love of Jesus with others?

Exploring the Mass

By his words and actions, Jesus Christ showed us God's unending love for us. We are given this love to share with others. We can be people of compassion like Jesus and reach out to other people. All of us need help some time in our lives.

The second reading from Scripture at Sunday Mass is from the New Testament letters (and sometimes in the Easter season from the Book of Revelation). We hear how the people of the early church lived their faith in Jesus Christ. They gathered together to celebrate the Eucharist and share what they had with those in need.

One second reading is from the Letter of Paul to the Ephesians 5:2. In this reading we hear proclaimed "Live in love, as Christ loved us." We are called to share the love of Jesus Christ with other people by what we do and say each day.

Learning activity

Role-play kindness to others

We can encourage children to live Scripture with role-play. Children act out ways they can be kind to others. Divide children into groups of three and give each group a situation.

Kindness role-plays

- Help a family member at home.
- Assist an elderly person.
- Welcome a new neighbor child.
- Include another child at recess.
- Share what you have with others.
- Reach out to a younger child.

Allow children a few minutes to discuss their role-play ideas. Then each group role-plays a way to be kind others using words and actions.

Children's take-home idea

We are called to share God's love with other people by our words and actions. This week, look for at least one opportunity to do an act of kindness for someone else without expecting a thank you.

Praying together

God of love,
we thank you for your love
and your many blessings.
Show us how to share your love
and your light with others.
Thank you for guiding our way
and being with us on our faith journey. Amen.

PART OF THE MASS:
Second Reading

FAMILY IDEAS

The second reading at Mass on Sundays is usually from the New Testament letters. We hear how the people of the early church followed Jesus Christ and shared the good news. We too are called to share the love of Jesus Christ with other people by our words and actions.

▶ Saint Teresa of Calcutta said, "Kind words can be short and easy to speak, but their echoes are truly endless." Talk as a family about using our words to build up people, not to tear them down. Our words have great power and can bring hope to the lives of others.

▶ Talk about ways we can be kind to others. Situations include helping a parent with dinner, making a card for a grandparent, playing a game with a younger child, welcoming a new child in your neighborhood, standing up for someone who is being called names at school, or helping an elderly neighbor.

FAMILY PRAYER

God of love, guide our family to follow you in our lives as the early Christians did in theirs. Show our family how to share your love and your light with others. Help us to be people of kindness and compassion. Amen.

Note to First Communion families

As children prepare for First Communion encourage them to be people of love for others as Jesus was. This is a great time for a family service project such as creating a soft fleece blanket for a child who is living in a shelter. Many websites show how to make a no-sew fleece blanket by tying knots.

Sing Out Alleluia

→ PART OF THE MASS: *Gospel Acclamation*

Catechist notes

We sing the Gospel Acclamation before the Gospel is proclaimed. For most of the church year this includes the Alleluia. (During Lent we do not proclaim the Alleluia; instead we proclaim "Glory and Praise to you, Lord Jesus Christ.")

Sharing question

Why do we sing the Alleluia before the Gospel at Mass?

Exploring the Mass

When it is time for the Gospel at Mass, we stand and get ready to greet our Lord Jesus Christ who is present in the Gospel. The word *alleluia* means "praise God!" We sing out "Alleluia, Alleluia" because we are about to hear the good news of Jesus Christ.

In his letter *The Joy of the Gospel*, Pope Francis said, "The joy of the Gospel fills the hearts and lives of all who encounter Jesus." We are called to be joyful people because we know the good news of Jesus Christ.

Learning activity

Craft a stained-glass window.

Many churches have stained glass windows that show us stories from the Bible or about the saints. Children can make a visual reminder to give praise by crafting a stained-glass window.

To begin this project, children make a church window shape by rounding the top of a sheet of colored craft foam with a scissors. Then they cut out a cross of another color and glue it in the middle. (Precut crosses are also available at craft stores if time is short.)

The stained-glass look comes from brightly colored pieces of self-stick craft foam cut into rectangles, squares, and triangles that are placed around the cross.

Children's take-home idea

Look for what is good in your life and in the world this week instead of what is negative. The more you look for good things, the more you will find them. As disciples of Jesus Christ, we are called to be joyful people.

Praying together

God of joy,
we praise you for all that you are
and all that you have done for us.
Together may we lift our hearts
and our voices as we proclaim Alleluia
at Mass and in our lives.
Amen. Alleluia!

PART OF THE MASS:
Gospel Acclamation

FAMILY IDEAS

When it is time for the Gospel, we stand to sing the Gospel Acclamation at Mass. For most of the year this is the Alleluia. The word *alleluia* means "praise God!" We know we will encounter Jesus Christ in the Gospel. We have much for which to praise God.

▶ Encourage family members to live in joy. Pope Francis said, "The joy of the gospel fills the hearts and lives of all who encounter Jesus" (*The Joy of the Gospel*, 2014). Talk about what this means to your family.

▶ Share ideas as a family of ways to be joyful people, such as saying good morning, finding the positive in each day, expressing appreciation for what others do, and watching for opportunities to help other people.

FAMILY PRAYER

God of joy, we praise you for all that you are and all that you have done for us. We lift up our voices that we may proclaim Alleluia at Mass and in our lives. Help our family to live in joy and see the blessings in each day. Amen. Alleluia!

Note to First Communion families

Preparing a child for First Communion should be a joyful time. Encourage your child to give thanks to God for the gift of the Eucharist and other blessings in their lives. Remind them that we are to share the joy of the gospel with others.

Walk with Jesus

→ ## PART OF THE MASS: *Gospel*

Catechist notes

Proclaiming the Gospel is the high point of the Liturgy of the Word. The gospel reading for each Sunday is in the Book of the Gospels, which is carried in the opening procession. We are called to live as gospel people.

Sharing question

What are the four gospels we hear proclaimed at Mass?

Exploring the Mass

We hear the gospels proclaimed in a three-year cycle. In year A, we hear from Matthew, in year B from Mark, and in year C from Luke. The Gospel of John is proclaimed on special feasts and during the Easter season. Through the gospels Jesus Christ continues to speak to us today as he did to his disciples. The word *gospel* means "good news."

The priest or the deacon proclaims the Gospel at Mass. After the Gospel, he says, "The Gospel of the Lord" and we respond, "Praise to you, Lord Jesus Christ." We are called to live as followers of Jesus at home, at church, at school, in our neighborhoods, and in our world.

Learning activity

Share ideas with "Be like Jesus" cards

One way to remember the example of Jesus in the gospels is with "Be Like Jesus" cards. Before gathering with the children, print on colored index card things Jesus did that we are to do also.

"Be like Jesus" cards

- Jesus took time to pray. When are times we can pray?
- Jesus helped people who were sick. How can we help people who are ill?
- Jesus had compassion for people. How can we extend a helping hand to others?
- Jesus forgave others. How can we show forgiveness to others?
- Jesus called his disciples. To whom can we tell the good news about Jesus?

Put all the cards in a basket. Have children take turns reading a card out loud to the group. Then all the children discuss ways we can be like Jesus. This activity encourages children to share their ideas with others and walk with Jesus each day.

Children's take-home idea

Rejoice because we know the good news of Jesus Christ. Read a gospel story this week from a children's Bible or watch an animated video on YouTube such as the story of the good Samaritan. Think about the message Jesus wants to share with you.

Praying together

Lord Jesus Christ,
we see in the four gospels
how you cared for all people.
Help us live the challenge of the gospels
and walk your way of love.
Amen.

PART OF THE MASS:
Gospel

FAMILY IDEAS

Through the gospels at Mass, Jesus Christ continues to speak to us just as he did to his first disciples. The word of God is for all generations. The word *gospel* means "good news." We hear each of the gospels proclaimed at Mass every three years. In year A we hear from Matthew, in year B from Mark, and in year C from Luke. The gospel of John is proclaimed during Christmas, the Easter season, and on special feasts throughout the year.

▶ Get a children's Bible that children can read themselves. Also provide Bible story books about Jesus with colorful pictures for your child's bookshelf. Then children have the option of sometimes choosing a Bible story as a bedtime story that a parent or grandparent reads to them.

▶ Brainstorm ideas as family to live as followers of Jesus at home, at church, at school, in your community, and in the world, such as contributing items to the local food pantry or donating school supplies to a family shelter. Choose one idea to do together.

FAMILY PRAYER

Lord Jesus Christ, open our hearts to your word in Scripture. Help our family follow you and live the challenge of the gospels. Guide us to walk your way of love together and make a difference for someone else this day. Amen.

Note to First Communion families

Children in preparation for First Communion should be familiar with Bible stories about Jesus and events of his life. Ask your child to tell you their favorite gospel story. After Mass, call the child's attention to what the gospel says about Jesus and about us.

Reflect on God's Word

→ PART OF THE MASS: *Homily*

Catechist notes

The word of God in Scripture speaks to our lives today. The homily helps us make the connection between Scripture and how we live it out. We reflect on how we can follow Jesus Christ and become the people God created us to be.

Sharing question

Why do we have a homily at Mass?

Exploring the Mass

The homily explores the Scripture readings of the day. Through the first and second reading and the gospel reading we are called to follow Jesus Christ. Scripture continues to speak to us through the actions of the Holy Spirit in our lives.

We sit and listen to the homily as the priest or deacon shares ideas on living our faith after we leave Mass. We must have open hearts and open minds so that we can see ways to build the kingdom of God for all people. Encourage the children to listen for one word or one idea in the homily that they can take with them.

Learning activity

Reach out with a placemat project

We are to reach out to other people as Jesus did. Do a project for people in the community who are not able to attend Mass because they are elderly or in poor health. Let children make placemats for an organization such as Meals on Wheels that delivers meals to homebound seniors.

Explain to children that these organizations not only provide food, but a visit from the volunteers. For some homebound people, the person delivering the meals may be the only person they talk to all day. Let children know that the placemats they make will be delivered by the organization with individual meals.

Use 12 x 18-inch construction paper. Provide materials for children to decorate the placemats with stickers, drawings, or cutout paper shapes. Depending on their age, let children create one or several placemats. Remind them that receiving a colorful, handmade placemat will let the people know that others care. Ask the children to pray for the people who will receive their placemats.

Children's take-home idea

Serve others as Jesus taught us by his words and example. Open your heart to the needs of others. This week help a family member, someone at school, or an organization that reaches out to people in need.

Praying together

Come, Holy Spirit,
into our hearts and our lives
as we reflect on the readings at Mass.
Help us to be a community of your people
who support one another
and live your word each day.
Amen.

PART OF THE MASS:
Homily

FAMILY IDEAS

The homily explores the Scripture readings of the Mass. The homily helps us make the connection between Scripture and how we live. We reflect on how we can become the people God created us to be.

▷ A question of the week about the Scripture readings helps families start talking. See if there is one in your parish bulletin or look online for publishers that offer this feature. Sharing about the Sunday readings is helpful to all family members.

▷ Talk about making choices. We cannot control what happens to us, but we can choose how we respond. We can ask God's help in dealing with difficult situations. We can guard against holding grudges. The better choice is one that helps us be who God created us to be.

FAMILY PRAYER

Come, Holy Spirit, into our hearts and lives as we reflect on the readings at Mass. Help our family to support one another and live your word each day. Together, may we reach out a helping hand to others. Amen.

Note to First Communion families

It is helpful for children preparing for First Communion to be familiar with the priests and deacons at your parish. This encourages children to be more involved. Take the time to stop and say hello to one of the priests or deacons after Mass.

Believe in God

→ ## PART OF THE MASS: *Profession of Faith*

Catechist notes

In the Profession of Faith, the Creed, we pro-claim what we believe. Together, we affirm our faith in God, who is Father, Son, and Holy Spirit. We are called to live what we believe. The Creed is proclaimed on Sundays and very important feast days.

Sharing question

What difference should faith in God make in our lives?

Exploring the Mass

At Mass we respond to the word of God in the readings with a statement of faith in God. We say the words of the Creed together as we recall all that God has done for us. God has a purpose for each of our lives. God also gives us the gifts to accomplish that purpose.

Being Catholic is more than a label. It is a way of life in which we walk with Jesus Christ. Our actions should show other people who God is. In the Creed we proclaim our belief in the Trinity: God who is Father and Creator, Son and Redeemer, and the Holy Spirit, who guides our church and our lives. By celebrating Sunday Mass together, the faith of each of us and the faith of all of us are strengthened.

Learning activity

Assemble a shamrock cross

A story about Saint Patrick says that he taught the people of Ireland about the Trinity by showing them a three-leaf clover and explain-ing that, just as there are three leaves on one shamrock, so there are three persons in one God—Father, Son, and Holy Spirit.

Show children how to make shamrock crosses. Each child cuts a cross shape about seven inches high out of green construction paper. Then children add several shamrock stickers to decorate their crosses.

Children's take-home idea

Put your faith in God into action this week. Live in faith, hope, and love of God and others. Ask the Holy Spirit to guide you to make good choices in your life so you can become all God created you to be.

Praying together

Wonderful God,
we believe in you, honor you,
and give you thanks.
Guide our hearts and lives
that we may live as you created us.
We pray in the name of the Father,
and of the Son, and of the Holy Spirit.
Amen.

PART OF THE MASS:
Profession of Faith

FAMILY IDEAS

At Mass we respond to the readings from Scripture with a profession of our faith in God. In the Creed we proclaim our belief in the Trinity: God, the Father and Creator; God, the Son and Redeemer; and God, the Holy Spirit, who guides our church and our lives. By celebrating the Mass together, the faith of each of us and the faith of all of us as a community are strengthened.

▶ Encourage children to look around them and see evidence of God in creation. There are billions of stars in our universe. Go outside at night and look at the stars in the sky. Get a book about stars from the library or visit a planetarium to learn about them.

▶ Explore the idea that we join our voices together in the Creed because we are a community of believers. We are also united in this statement of faith with the people who have gone before us and those who will come after us. We are the people of God.

FAMILY PRAYER

Wonderful God, we believe in you and honor you. Help our family to live what we believe each day and to share the good news of Jesus Christ with others. We pray in the name of the Father, and of the Son, and of the Holy Spirit. Amen.

Note to First Communion families

This is a great time to start a new family tradition and keep it going after First Communion. For example, if you do not already say grace before meals, start now. Print off a copy and post it in the kitchen as a reminder.

Lord, Hear Our Prayer

➥ PART OF THE MASS: *Prayer of the Faithful*

Catechist notes

In the Prayer of the Faithful we offer prayers to God on behalf of the needs of others. We pray for the whole church, for the world, for the local community, and for people in need. We are also called to put our prayers into action. God sends us to help others.

Sharing question

Who are people who need our prayers?

Exploring the Mass

At Mass we pray for the needs of other people in the Prayer of the Faithful. Some of the people we pray for include the homeless, the hungry, and the sick. We join our prayers with people around the world. Celebrating the Mass connects us to God and to one another.

Each petition usually ends with the deacon or lector saying, "We pray to the Lord." We respond to each prayer with "Lord, hear our prayer," or another suitable response. We can also add our own individual prayers for others silently at this time of the Mass. With God's help we can make a difference in the lives of others.

Learning activity

Pray with prayer sticks

Encourage children to pray for the needs of other people with a prayer stick activity. Before the children arrive, print on colorful wooden craft sticks the names of people to pray for.

Be sure to have enough sticks so each child will have one. Put all the sticks in an empty can.

Prayer sticks

refugees • mentally ill • elderly • sick lonely • families • homeless • in the hospital grieving a loss • victims of violence hungry • people in war-torn countries

When the children gather, explore the idea that we are called to pray for the needs of other people. Pass the can and let each child take a prayer stick. The first child reads his or her petition to the group saying, "For the homeless…" and all the children respond, "Lord, hear our prayer." Remind the children to pray for others not only at Mass but also at other times throughout the week.

Children's take-home idea

Take time this week to pray for people in need in our world. Each of us is called to pray for the needs of others. Each day pray for a different person or group. Ask other people to pray too. Then put your prayers into action.

Praying together

God of compassion,
we pray for people living in poverty
and for children who go to bed hungry at night.
We pray for the sick, those who are injured,
the homeless, and people in hospitals.
Help us to reach out a helping hand
to people in need with your love and comfort.
Amen.

PART OF THE MASS:
Prayer of the Faithful

FAMILY IDEAS

In the Prayer of the Faithful at Mass, we offer prayers to God for the needs of others. We pray for the church, for the world, for our leaders, for people living in poverty, for those who do not have enough to eat, for people facing illness, for those grieving the loss of a loved one, and others. We can also add our own individual prayers silently in our hearts.

➤ Encourage children to pray for the needs of others not only at Mass but at other times too. When you hear an ambulance siren, ask family members to take a moment and pray for the person who needs help.

➤ Make a family prayer calendar. Write down a different person or group to pray for each week. Then on Sundays, say a short prayer for that intention. Simply add the prayer for the people in need right after saying grace before dinner.

FAMILY PRAYER

God of compassion, we pray for the elderly, for people living in poverty, for the sick, and for children who go to bed hungry at night. May our family find a way to reach out to people who need help. May others see your love for them through our actions. Amen.

Note to First Communion families

First Communion children should learn to pray not only for our own needs but for the needs of other people, even those they do not know. God created us to be a community that prays for one another and cares about one another. Teach your children that God sends us to help others.

Give Thanks to God

➜ PART OF THE MASS: *Liturgy of the Eucharist*

Catechist notes

We come together at the Liturgy of the Eucharist to give thanks to the God of all of us. We celebrate who God is in our lives and who we are as God's people. We give thanks to God for all God has done for us and for God's love for each of us.

Sharing question

What are some things for which we can give thanks to God?

Exploring the Mass

The third part of the Mass is the Liturgy of the Eucharist. Explore with the children some of the many gifts our God has given us, such as sunshine and stars, oceans and mountains, animals and people, music and laughter, and most of all, God's love for us. The word *eucharist* means "thanksgiving."

In the Liturgy of the Eucharist, we thank God for all God has done for us. Together we offer the gift of Jesus Christ to the Father through the Holy Spirit.

The Liturgy of the Eucharist has the following parts:

Presentation of gifts	Great Amen
Prayer over the offerings	Our Father
Preface	Sign of peace
Holy, holy, holy	Communion
Eucharistic prayer	Prayer after Communion
Consecration	

Learning activity

Do a church visit

Guide children in learning about the main parts of the Mass by a visit to the church. Give them a close-up view of where Mass takes place. This activity will be a learning experience for some children and a review for others.

Make the church visit as interactive as possible. As they enter the church, let them make the sign of the cross with holy water as a reminder of their baptism. Show them the ambo, where the word of God in Scripture is proclaimed. Let them stand at the altar and see candles, the cross, and any other Mass items that are available. Point out the tabernacle and explain how it holds the consecrated Body of Christ. Encourage children to ask questions as you go.

Children's take-home idea:

Celebrate God's many gifts in your life. Each day this week, give thanks to God for five blessings. Try to think of different things each day. Praying prayers of thanksgiving to God at bedtime is a great way to end each day.

Praying together

God of all generations,
we give you thanks for all you have done for us
and for your unending love for each of us.
Help us to offer our prayers together at Mass
and live each day with faith, hope, and love.
Amen.

PART OF THE MASS: Liturgy of the Eucharist

FAMILY IDEAS

We come together at the Liturgy of the Eucharist to give thanks to the God of all of us. The word *eucharist* means "thanksgiving." We give thanks at Mass to God for all God has done for us and for God's great love for each of us.

▶ Take a walk or a hike as a family and admire the beauty of God's creation. As a family, talk about the wonders of creation and the people who care about us. Give thanks to God for all that God has done for us.

▶ Talk with your children about why we stand and kneel at Mass. We stand as a sign of honor before the God who gives us life and all blessings. We kneel in adoration during the Eucharistic Prayer as the bread and wine become the Body and Blood of Christ. (For more information see the Prayer and Worship page on the U.S. bishops' website: usccb.org)

FAMILY PRAYER

God of all generations, thank you for being here with our family today and giving us the gift of one another. Guide us to worship together at Sunday Mass with our parish community. May we live each day with faith in you, hope in the future, and love for all people. Amen.

Note to First Communion families

If you have a child with special needs, he or she can prepare to receive First Communion also. Check with your parish director of faith formation. Resources are also available from the National Catholic Partnership on Disability at ncpd.org. This includes a First Eucharist preparation kit and resources such as a picture missal of the Mass.

Offer Gifts to Our God

➥ PART OF THE MASS: *Presentation of Gifts*

Catechist notes

The Liturgy of the Eucharist begins with a song and the offering of the gifts of bread and wine. We offer these gifts and ourselves to God. The bread and wine are placed on the altar, and we pray that all our gifts will be pleasing to our God.

Sharing question

What gifts are brought forward in the gifts procession?

Exploring the Mass

People in the parish bring forward our gifts of bread and wine along with the collection basket. These people represent all of us. We also offer our hearts, our lives, and our actions to the God who created us and loves us. The bread and wine are placed on the altar. They will become the Body and Blood of Christ. The priest prays over the bread and wine. We respond, "Blessed be God for ever." What a wonderful prayer this is!

Learning activity

Draw Mass prayer posters

In the Mass we offer to God the Father the gift of God's own Son, Jesus Christ, through the Holy Spirit. We also offer to God all that we are, and we ask God for what we need to live as disciples of Jesus Christ. Explore with the children some prayers at Mass that help us praise God. The children can make colorful posters of Mass prayers and decorate them.

Mass prayers for posters

Glory to God in the highest
    (Glory to God)
Praise to You, Lord Jesus Christ
    (response to Gospel)
Blessed are you, Lord God of all creation
    (over the bread and wine)
Blessed be God forever
    (preparation of gifts)
Thanks be to God
    (end of Mass)

Display the Mass posters where others can be reminded of the beautiful prayers we pray together at Mass. Explain to the children that these prayers can be used in our lives during the week too.

Children's take-home idea

Choose one of the short prayers from Mass that you heard about today and pray it during this coming week. A prayer can be just one sentence, such as "Blessed be God forever." You can pray in your own words too.

Praying together

Faithful God,
when the bread and wine
are brought forward at Mass,
we offer ourselves to you also.
Bless our gifts and bless our lives
and all those who gather together
to celebrate in your holy name.
Amen.

PART OF THE MASS:
Presentation of Gifts

FAMILY IDEAS

The Liturgy of the Eucharist begins with a song. People in the parish bring forward our gifts of bread and wine and the collection basket. The priest places the bread and wine on the altar and prays that our gifts at Mass will be pleasing to our God. We respond, "Blessed be God for ever."

▶ The people bringing up the gifts of bread and wine represent all of us. Along with these gifts, which will be transformed in the Body and Blood of Christ, we offer our hearts, our lives, and our actions to God, praying that we too may be transformed by the Holy Spirit into the body of Christ on earth.

▶ The money given in the collection is used to support the priests, parish ministries, and the parish facilities. But stewardship is not just financial. We are to offer our time, our talents, and our treasure to our church. Talk as a family about ways to do all three.

FAMILY PRAYER

Faithful God, we give you praise and thanks for all you have done for us. Guide our hearts and lives that we may live as disciples of Jesus Christ in all that we do. Bless our family, and bless all those who gather with us at Mass as we celebrate in your holy name. Amen.

Note to First Communion families

Participating in the Mass is an important part of First Communion preparation. Consider volunteering as a gift family to carry the bread, wine, and collection basket at a Sunday Mass. Look at your parish website for contact information or find another way to be involved. This helps children understand that they are part of the parish community.

Join Our Prayers Together

→ **PART OF THE MASS: *Prayer over the Offerings***

Catechist notes

The short prayer over the offerings that the priest says is different each Sunday. Prayer is an important part of who we are at Mass and during the week. Prayer connects us to God. The Mass is the supreme prayer of our Catholic faith.

Sharing question

What are times we can pray to God?

Exploring the Mass

We pray at Mass, and we can pray at other times too. We can pray when we are happy or sad. We can give thanks to God or ask for God's forgiveness. We can pray in the morning, at night, and in between too. We turn to God in prayer because we know we can trust God.

The priest prays over the offerings of bread and wine on the altar. We ask God to accept our offerings. The presider says, "Through Christ our Lord" and we respond, "Amen."

Learning activity

Take part in a Jesus meditation

One way children can pray beyond the Mass is with a Jesus meditation. This helps children open their hearts and lives to Jesus in prayer. Ask the children to close their eyes. Then slowly read the meditation:

See yourself on a hillside. The sun is shining and the sky is blue. You are surprised to see Jesus in the distance. Then he walks toward you. Jesus smiles and sits down next to you. You know that Jesus loves and cares about you.

You turn to Jesus and tell him what is going on in your life. You share your problems and worries with him. Jesus listens quietly to you. Feel his love for you in your heart. What does Jesus say to you? Listen to his words.

Now come back to this time and place. Hold the peace that Jesus gives you in your heart. You can always talk to Jesus, and he will listen.

Children's take-home idea

Open your heart to God this week. Talk to God about what is going on in your life, and share your hopes and dreams. Prayer is an important part of our relationship with our God. Through prayer we recognize God's presence and love in our lives.

Praying together

God of all times and places,
we give glory and honor to you
as we celebrate your love for us.
May we be people of prayer at Mass
and in all that we do each day.
Blessed be God forever.
Amen.

PART OF THE MASS: **Prayer over the Offerings**

FAMILY IDEAS

At Mass, the short prayer over the offerings that the priest says is different each Sunday. This prayer ends when the priest says, "Through Christ our Lord." We respond "Amen" and make the prayer our own. Prayer connects us to our God. Prayer is part of who we are and who we are called to be.

▶ Stress to your children that there are many ways to pray to God after we leave Mass. We can pray in the morning and at night, in our own words or with traditional prayers, when we are happy, sad, or afraid. We can pray by ourselves or with our family.

▶ Pray with your children when you tuck them in at night. This helps them become people of prayer who praise God and ask God's help in their lives. Prayer is an important part of our relationship with God. Teach your children not only traditional prayers, but also how to pray in their own words.

FAMILY PRAYER

God of all times and places, we lift up our hearts and voices to praise you. Thank you for the gift of our family, and help us support one another in all things. May we be people of prayer at Mass and in all that we do each day. Blessed be God forever. Amen.

Note to First Communion families

Prayer is an essential part of preparing a child for First Communion. Pray for God's help in guiding your child. Pray with your child as a family. Give thanks to God for blessings. Encourage your child to praise God. Keep prayer meaningful for children by praying in many different ways.

Lift Up Our Hearts

→ PART OF THE MASS: *Eucharistic Prayer*

Catechist notes

To begin the Eucharistic Prayer, the priest says three phrases, and we respond to each one. The first is "The Lord be with you." These prayers and our responses remind us that God is always with us. The Eucharistic Prayer is central to our faith and the Mass.

Sharing question

What does the word "Eucharist" mean?

Exploring the Mass

The word *eucharist* is from a Greek work that means "thanksgiving" or "giving thanks." God created everything in our world out of love for us. God also created us, redeemed us, and lives in us. We give God thanks at Mass for all the gifts we receive from God. We should also thank God each day during the week.

The Eucharistic Prayer is the most important part of the Mass. The priest offers the prayer to God the Father in the name of all of us. We remember that we are a eucharistic people. We join our prayers with the prayers of people all over the world who are celebrating Mass and praising God. The more we are open to God in our lives, the more God will be able to work through us.

Learning activity

Give thanks with picture cards

Before gathering with the children, assemble small pictures of God's creation. Pictures can be from magazines or online. Look for people, flowers, mountains, food, and animals. Glue each picture to a colored index card for durability. Put the cards in a basket.

Encourage the children to give thanks to God for all the gifts God has given us. Pass the basket around the circle, and let each child select a picture card. Then each child in turn thanks God for what is in the picture he or she chose. This gives children experience in praising God and helps them be more aware of the many gifts God has given us. They also get experience in praying in their own words.

Children's take-home idea

God is with us at all times and places of our lives. We can see God's presence in the world and the people God created. Take time this week to notice the beauty and wonder of the world God gave to us. Share these blessings with others so that they can praise God too.

Praying together

God of all creation,
we give you our unending praise
for making a world filled with miracles.
Help us to give thanks to you
through the Eucharistic Prayer
and how we live our lives.
Amen.

Part of the Mass:
Eucharistic Prayer

FAMILY IDEAS

The Eucharistic Prayer is the most important part of the Mass. In it, we remember that our God created us, redeemed us, and lives in us. We should give thanks and praise to God at Sunday Mass and in our lives during the week too.

▶ Make a family gratitude chain in seasonal colors. Cut colorful construction paper or scrapbook paper into strips. Family members write things for which they are thankful on several of the strips. Loop the chain together with tape. Hang it up as a reminder to give thanks to God each day.

▶ Go on a walk or a hike and point out the beautiful things God has made for us. This includes flowers, rivers, rocks, trees, sunlight, and people. Marvel out loud at what an awesome and loving God we have to make such a wonderful world for us. Later talk about what family members liked best.

FAMILY PRAYER

God of all creation, we give you praise for creating a world filled with wonders. Thank you for your love for each of us and for the love we share as a family. Help us to give thanks to you through the Eucharistic Prayer at Mass and how we live each day. Amen.

Note to First Communion families

Look for pictures of your child's baptism and share them with your child who is getting ready for First Communion. Remind your child that every time we make the sign of the cross with holy water at Mass, we remember our baptism. We are to live as followers of Jesus Christ in all ways.

Thank God for Sending Jesus

➡ PART OF THE MASS: *Preface*

Catechist notes

We are called to praise God, who loves us without end. The words of the Preface remind us that God sent a Redeemer to us out of love. The priest chooses from several prefaces at Mass, based on the church year.

Sharing question

How did God keep the promise to send us a Savior?

Exploring the Mass

In the Preface at Mass, we give thanks to God. We celebrate that God kept the promise to send a Savior to us. This promise was fulfilled in a way no one could have expected because Jesus Christ is the Son of God. Explain to the children that we should give praise and thanks for all that God has done for us. Talk with the learners about some of God's promises to us in Scripture.

God's promises in Scripture

The Lord God is with you wherever you go.
    (Joshua 1:9)
I have called you by name, you are mine.
    (Isaiah 43:1)
You shall be my people and I will be your God.
    (Jeremiah 30:22)
Come to me…and I will give you rest.
    (Matthew 11:28–29)
Peace I leave with you; my peace I give to you.
    (John 14:27)

Learning activity

Put together a "God's promises" craft

Stress to the children that we can believe in God's promises. Show them how to make a colorful promise craft. Provide copies of some of God's promises on a variety of colors of copy paper. Cut the pages into individual verses.

On a sheet of paper, each child prints the words "God's promises" in the middle. Then the children choose promises to glue to their papers. Encourage the children to share God's promises with their families.

Children's take-home idea

Trust in God even when life is difficult. God is always with us and keeps the promises made to the people. Thank God this week for sending Jesus Christ to us as a Savior and all that God has done for us.

Praying together

God of promises,
we give you thanks and praise
that you keep your promises to your people.
May we trust always in your word
and live as your holy people in all we do.
Amen.

PART OF THE MASS:
Preface

FAMILY IDEAS

In the Preface at Mass we celebrate that God fulfilled the promise to the people and sent a Savior—Jesus Christ, the Son of God. This promise was fulfilled in a way no one could have expected. God keeps promises to us. We are called to trust always in our God. Nurture an attitude of gratitude in your family:

▷ At the dinner table ask each person to say something for which they are thankful that day. This might be friends, learning something new, someone who helped them, a sunny day, a puppy, or even having pizza for dinner.

▷ Make a "Thank you, God" sign for your home or print off a psalm verse poster from the internet, such as "I give thanks to you, O Lord my God, with my whole heart" (Psalm 86:12). Frame it and place on a shelf where every family member will see it and remember to give thanks to God.

FAMILY PRAYER

God of promises, we give you thanks and praise for always keeping your promises to us. We are your people, and you are our God. We know that you are with us in all things. Guide our family to trust always in you and in your love for us. Amen.

Note to First Communion families

A great idea to help prepare your child for First Communion is a family activity that helps others. We show God we are grateful for what we have by sharing with others. One family project is to make "thinking of you" cards and deliver them to people at a care center. (Call before you go.)

Give Honor to the Lord

➜ PART OF THE MASS: *Holy, Holy, Holy*

Catechist notes

At Mass we sing together the prayer of praise that begins, "Holy, holy, holy." We are created by God and are to give glory to God. As the Eucharistic Prayer continues, we open our hearts and our lives to God.

Sharing question

How can we praise God in our lives?

Exploring the Mass

By our words and our actions, we give praise to our awesome God. In the "Holy, Holy, Holy" prayer at Mass we join our voices in song as we honor God. The first part of this prayer comes from the cry of the angel in Isaiah 6:3. The second part comes from the gospel story of Jesus' entry into Jerusalem. In Matthew 21:9 we hear "Blessed is the one who comes in the name of the Lord! Hosanna in the highest." These words of Scripture echo down to the present day.

Learning activity

Play a word guess game

Help children become familiar with the vocabulary of the Mass with a word guess activity. This catches their attention while they review the words.

On a white board, put one dash for each letter of the first word or phrase. If there are multiple words, leave a space between each one. Ask young people to guess letters in the words one letter at a time. Fill in correct letters as they are guessed. Each child gets only one turn at a time.

When the word or words have been guessed correctly, fill in the remaining letters. Remind the children what the word refers to in the Mass. Then move on to the next word. Reviewing with a game engages children's interest and helps them understand difficult words in the Mass.

Mass words for word guess game

Responsorial Psalm	Lord's Prayer	Creed
Prayer of the Faithful	Consecration	Blessing
Sign of the Cross	First Reading	Gospel
Eucharistic Prayer	Sign of Peace	Communion
Lord, have mercy	Opening Prayer	Greeting
Gospel Acclamation	Glory to God	Preface
Second Reading	Holy, holy, holy	Homily

Children's take-home idea

Remember that God will always love you. We should put God first in our lives and live as Jesus showed us. Make more time for prayer this week by spending less time on something else. Our choices should help us live as disciples of Jesus Christ.

Praying together

Jesus, Savior of the world,
we lift up our hearts and our voices
to give praise to your holy name
at Mass and in our lives.
May we walk with you each day
and give glory to you in all we do. Amen.

PART OF THE MASS:
Holy, Holy, Holy

FAMILY IDEAS

We sing together at Mass the prayer of praise that begins, "Holy, holy, holy." We are created by God and can give praise and honor to God by our words and our actions. As the Eucharistic Prayer continues, we open our hearts and lives to God. We should put God first each day.

▶ Take advantage of everyday-life moments to remind children that God loves us and is always with us. Draw their attention to a beautiful sunset, a rainbow, a seashell, corn growing in a farmer's field, or people who care about them.

▶ We honor God when we live as God created us to live. The beautiful Peace Prayer written in the spirit of Saint Francis teaches us how to be disciples of Jesus Christ. It begins "Lord, make me an instrument of your peace: where there is hatred, let me sow love." Pray this prayer as a family and talk about ways your family can put the words into action.

FAMILY PRAYER

Jesus, Savior of the world, thank you for coming as a Savior for each of us and for all people. Help our family walk with you in faith and give glory to your name in all that we do. May we lift up our voices in prayer to you at Mass and during the week. Amen.

Note to First Communion families

Be sure your child knows some stories of some saints. We all need heroes, and saints are examples of faith for us. Help your First Communion child learn about a saint for whom they are named, a saint whose feast day is on their birthday, or a saint whose story speaks to their lives.

Jesus Is with Us

→ PART OF THE MASS: *Consecration*

Catechist notes

There are four Eucharistic Prayers that are usually used for Sunday Mass. We ask God to send the Holy Spirit so that the bread and wine will become Jesus. The Eucharist is the heart of the church's life.

Sharing question

Why did Jesus Christ give us the Eucharist?

Exploring the Mass

The Eucharist is a sign of God's continuing love for us. The bread and wine become the Eucharist, the Body and Blood of Christ, at the consecration. This miracle happens at each Mass all over the world.

The Eucharist unites us with Jesus Christ and with one another. The Eucharist is the central part of the Mass. The *Catechism of the Catholic Church* tells us that "The Eucharist is the source and summit of the Christian life" (1324).

Learning activity

Create a chalice and host craft

Children can make a craft to remind them that Jesus gives us the gift of himself in the Eucharist. Before gathering with the children, print Eucharist on a piece of paper, and underneath it print, "This is my body…this is my blood" (Matthew 26:26–28). Make a copy for each child.

Ask each child to cut out a chalice from gold scrapbook paper and glue it to an individual sheet of green paper. Then the child cuts out a white circle from an unlined index card. The circle is glued at the top of the chalice. Each child adds a cross sticker to the host to remind them that the Eucharist is Jesus. Finally, the children glue the words of consecration to the front of their individual chalices.

Children's take-home idea

Thank Jesus for the gift of his presence in the Eucharist. Look this week for ways to serve others as Jesus taught us. Help someone at home, at school, or in your community. We are to live as people of the Eucharist, sharing the love of Jesus with others.

Praying together

Jesus Christ, Lord, and Redeemer,
we thank you for the gift of the Eucharist,
in which you are always with us
through the action of the Holy Spirit.
Help us to remember that the Eucharist
commits us to following your way of love
in our lives each day.
Amen.

PART OF THE MASS:
Consecration

FAMILY IDEAS

The Eucharist is a sign of God's love for us and strengthens us for our faith journey. Through the Holy Spirit, the bread and wine become the body and blood of Jesus at Mass. This miracle happens over and over again. We thank God for all that God has done for us. The Eucharist unites us with Jesus Christ and with one another.

▶ The consecration is the most holy part of the Mass. Be sure family members are attentive to what is happening on the altar. Focus on Jesus Christ, who is present in the bread and wine. Give thanks to God for this great gift.

▶ Share with your children that God has a plan for each of our lives. It is a purpose only we can do. God gives us gifts so that we can serve one another. Help your children discover their gifts and how they can share them with others as God intended.

FAMILY PRAYER

Jesus Christ, Lord and Redeemer, we thank you for the gift of the Eucharist in which you are always with us. Help us to remember that the Eucharist commits us to follow your way of love and live as your disciples each day. Teach our family to be people who love others in your name. Amen.

Note to First Communion families

Stress to your child that First Communion is only the beginning of a special relationship with Jesus Christ in the Eucharist. Each time we receive Jesus Christ is special, not just the first time. The Eucharist is food that strengthens us for our faith journey throughout our lives.

Rejoice in Our God

→ PART OF THE MASS: *Great Amen*

Catechist notes

As the Eucharistic Prayer continues, the presider speaks in the name of all of us. In this part of the Mass we praise God, and we remember that the Father sent us Jesus Christ through the work of the Holy Spirit. Our "amen" concludes the Eucharistic Prayer.

Sharing question

What does the word "amen" mean?

Exploring the Mass

At the conclusion of the Eucharistic Prayer, the priest prays a prayer of praise to our God, ending with, "All glory and honor is yours for ever and ever." We say "Amen," which means "so be it." This amen is our yes to what was prayed by the priest in the name of us all.

We know that Jesus Christ is present in the Eucharist. We know that the Holy Spirit lives in us. We ask God to accept our offering of the Body and Blood of Jesus. We pray for people who have died and ask the saints to pray to God for us. We rejoice in all God has done for us.

Learning activity

Make "Thank you, God" notes

Remind the young people that the word *eucharist* means giving thanks. During the Eucharistic Prayer we thank God for all God has done for us. Place a sign on a wall or on poster board that says, "Thank you, God" in big letters.

Talk with the children about things for which we can give thanks to God. Encourage the children to think of ideas such as God's love, sunshine, rivers, mountains, trees, animals, and people who love us. Ask the children to print some of these ideas on colorful sticky notes and add them under the "Thank you, God" sign.

This project keeps children engaged and helps them feel that they are a part of the group. Many children are visual learners and need to see things as well as hear them in order to learn.

Children's take-home idea

Rejoice in God's unending love for you. Thank someone this week who has shared their faith in God with you. You can do this in person or by writing a note to that person. Tell someone else about God's love for them too.

Praying together

Amazing God,
we raise up our hearts and voices to you
and rejoice in all that you have done for us.
Through the Holy Spirit we offer the gift
of our Lord Jesus Christ present in the Eucharist.
May we give you praise in all we say and do.
Amen.

Part of the Mass:
Great Amen

FAMILY IDEAS

As the Eucharistic Prayer continues, the priest prays in the name of all of us. He asks God to accept our offering. The prayer to God concludes, "All glory and honor is yours for ever and ever." We respond "Amen," which means "so be it" or "yes." This amen is our "yes" to what was prayed by the priest in the name of us all.

▶ Share stories of hope and joy with your children. These can be personal stories or stories from a TV news program, newspaper, online news source, or magazine. Good things are happening in our communities. We can choose to look for the positive in life and pass on that hope to our children.

▶ Remember to express love and appreciation to one another in your family. Also take time to listen to each other. Remind your children that God always loves them. Only when people feel loved are they able to share love with others.

FAMILY PRAYER

Amazing God, we give glory to your holy name and rejoice in all that you have done for us. Through the Holy Spirit we offer the gift of our Lord Jesus Christ in the Eucharist. May our family give you praise in all we say and do, and may we live always in faith, in hope, and in love. Amen.

Note to First Communion families

Encourage your child to receive both the consecrated bread and the wine at First Communion and thereafter. This is how Jesus did it at the Last Supper with his disciples. It is the fullest expression of what the sacrament means.

Prayer of Jesus

➦ PART OF THE MASS: *Lord's Prayer*

Catechist notes

The communion rite begins with all of us praying the Lord's Prayer, which is also known as the Our Father. We are called to faith in God, who is the Father of all people. We are to live this prayer in our lives.

Sharing question

What is the prayer Jesus taught us?

Exploring the Mass

We pray together the Our Father at each Mass. This is the prayer that Jesus taught his disciples. The Our Father reminds us of our relationship with God and with one another. God is the Father of all people, and we must treat all people with dignity and respect.

Each of us is called to work to bring about God's kingdom for all people. We ask God to forgive us as we forgive others. The *Catechism of the Catholic Church* reminds us that "the Lord's Prayer is truly the summary of the whole gospel" (2761). We are called to live this prayer in our daily lives.

Learning activity

Join in an Our Father scramble

Before gathering with the children, print each phrase in the Our Father on a separate sheet of paper in large letters.

Ask ten children to volunteer for this activity and stand in front of the group. Mix up the phrases and give a sheet to each of the children. Ask the children to put themselves in the order of this prayer. Then each child reads their phrase in order.

Phrases for Our Father scramble

Our Father, who art in heaven,
hallowed be thy name;
thy kingdom come,
thy will be done on earth as it is in heaven.
Give us this day our daily bread,
and forgive us our trespasses,
as we forgive those who trespass against us;
and lead us not into temptation,
but deliver us from evil.
Amen.

Children's take-home idea

Treat other people with respect this week no matter what their age, color, nationality, or ability. All people are created and loved by God. Each of us is called to help bring about the kingdom of God by who we are and how we relate to other people.

Praying together

God, our Father,
we thank you for being the Father
of all nations and all people.
Help us to treat other people
with dignity and respect as your creation.
Amen.

PART OF THE MASS:
Our Father

FAMILY IDEAS

We pray together the Our Father at every Mass. All of us are on this journey to the Father together. Jesus taught us to call God our Father because all of us are created in God's image and likeness. The Our Father reminds us of our relationship with God and with one another. The Our Father gives us a plan for our lives.

▷ The Our Father is to be lived in our lives. It is a summary of the gospels. God is the Father of all people, and all are to be treated with dignity and respect. Jesus came for all people, all races, and all nations. Encourage all family members to speak respectfully of others.

▷ We memorize prayers so that we can pray them as a community and so we can pray when no words will come. Children should learn the Our Father, the Hail Mary, the Glory Be, and an Act of Contrition or Sorrow. They should also pray in their own words.

FAMILY PRAYER

God, our Father, we thank you for being the Father of all nations and all people. Help us to treat all people with dignity and respect in your name. May our family honor you by the way we share your love with others each day. Amen.

Note to First Communion families

Children preparing for First Communion should not only know the Our Father but understand that it is to be lived in our daily lives. We are to show respect for other people as God's creation. We are to forgive others as God forgives us. Talk about these ideas with your child as the opportunity arises.

Be Peacemakers

→ PART OF THE MASS: *Sign of Peace*

Catechist notes

Peace sometimes seems to be in short supply in our lives and in our world. Hopefully, after we leave Mass, we will continue to bring the peace of Jesus Christ to other people. We are all called to be peacemakers.

Sharing question

Why do we offer each other a sign of peace at Mass?

Exploring the Mass

We turn to those around us at Mass and offer a sign of peace as Jesus did to his disciples after his resurrection. We say, "Peace be with you" as Jesus did that day (John 20:19). He forgave those who had run away when he was crucified. Talk with the children about ways to live in peace in our lives. Give them examples, and ask the children to share their own ideas too.

Living as peacemakers

- Listen to what others have to say.
- Let go of grudges.
- Think of creative solutions to problems.
- Say something nice instead of something mean.
- Forgive someone who hurt you.
- Ignore a child who calls you names.
- Learn about people of other cultures.

Pope Francis reminds us that "peace is a daily commitment." Discuss what this means for us. We are to work for peace in our lives, in our communities, and in our world. We are to be peacemakers in our lives each day. We are all on this faith journey together.

Learning activity

Work together on a peace poster

Children can make a poster together to remember to live in peace. Print the words "Live in peace" on a sheet of poster board. Have each of the children draw around their hand on colorful construction paper. Ask the children to print one way they will live in peace on their hand shape. The children then cut out their hand shapes and glue them to the poster. Display the poster where the children will see it as a reminder to live in peace.

Children's take-home idea

We are called to turn away from selfishness and toward love for others. In this way, we live as Jesus calls us to do. Look for opportunities this week to be a peacemaker in family, your school, and your neighborhood.

Praying together

God of peace,
we pray today to be people of peace
in our communities, our country,
and our world.
We pray that there may be an end
to hatred, discrimination, and war.
May we learn to put aside differences
and work together for the good of all people.
Amen.

PART OF THE MASS:
Sign of Peace

FAMILY IDEAS

At Mass, we share a sign of peace with those around us. Jesus offered a sign of peace to his disciples after his resurrection. Jesus forgave those who had run away and denied him. He said to them, "Peace be with you" (John 20:19). We can bring peace to the lives of others—one person and one action at a time.

▶ Encourage family members to focus on what others do right, instead of what they do wrong. This helps children see something positive in a person or situation. This takes effort. Pope Francis reminds us that "peace is a daily commitment." Talk about what this means.

▶ Help your children think of peaceful actions they can do, such as letting go of grudges, listening carefully to others, refraining from judging people, or standing up for a child who is being bullied. Peace begins one step at a time. What we begin at Mass, we continue during the week.

FAMILY PRAYER

God of peace, help our family to be peacemakers in our communities, our country, and our world. We pray that there may be an end to hatred and violence. May we learn to put aside differences and focus on what is good in other people. Amen.

Note to First Communion families

Peace is to be lived in our lives as individuals, as a community, and as a world. Explore the idea as a family that we cannot control what happens to us, but we can control how we react. Children old enough for First Communion can learn to choose to live in love as Jesus showed us.

→ PART OF THE MASS: *Communion*

Catechist notes

As the time of receiving the Eucharist comes near, the priest and people together say, "Lord, I am not worthy that you should enter under my roof, but only say the word and my soul shall be healed." These words are based on the words of the centurion in Luke 7:6–7.

Sharing question

When did Jesus give us the Eucharist?

Exploring the Mass

Jesus gave us the gift of the Eucharist at the Last Supper before he died. Receiving the Eucharist strengthens us to live as Jesus did. In coming forward to Communion, we are united with Jesus Christ and with one another. The Eucharist commits us to serving other people during the week as we go about our lives.

When we receive Communion, we say "Amen," which is an act of faith. This "Amen" means we know that the bread and wine of the Eucharist are the Body and Blood of Jesus. Eucharist is not about us but about God's amazing love for us.

Let children know that Communion is taken to the people of the parish who are sick or elderly and are unable to participate in the Mass. Members of the parish community go to homes and hospitals to do this.

Learning activity

Make a Eucharist prayer card

It is important to help children take what they learn about the Mass into their lives beyond the classroom. We are to live what we believe. A simple way to do this is to let children make Eucharist prayer cards to take home.

Make a copy of the prayer below for each child. Show children how to glue the prayer to a larger piece of colorful card stock. Then they decorate the prayer by adding a cross and heart stickers on the left and right sides. Ask children to use the prayer card to pray to Jesus at home.

Children's take-home idea

Remember that the Eucharist calls us to love others in the name of Jesus. Look for a way to reach out to people in need this week. Be part of a parish or community project or think of your own idea. Share your idea with your family.

Praying together

Lord Jesus Christ,
at the Last Supper with your disciples
you gave us the amazing gift of the Eucharist.
May we grow in faith, hope, and love
each time we receive Communion.
Guide us to live as people of the Eucharist
and serve others each day as you did. Amen.

PART OF THE MASS:
Communion

FAMILY IDEAS

At the Last Supper on the night before he died, Jesus gave us the gift of the Eucharist. We don't have to earn this gift. The Eucharist is freely given to us out of God's love for each of us. In coming forward to Communion, we are united with Jesus Christ and with one another. After we receive Communion, we kneel to thank God in our hearts and ask for the help we need to live as Jesus taught us.

▶ Stress to children that God loves each of them with an unending love. The gift of the Eucharist is a gift given out of God's love for us. Encourage children to be open to the possibilities in life. Our past does not determine our future. All things are possible with God.

▶ The Eucharist commits us to serving others. As a family, share ways to do this, such as visiting someone in a care center, helping children in need in the community, and saying something kind instead of being critical.

FAMILY PRAYER

Lord Jesus Christ, at the Last Supper with your disciples you gave us the amazing gift of your presence in the Eucharist. Help us to serve others, just as you were the servant of all. We ask you to bless our family and help us live as your disciples each day. Amen.

Note to First Communion families

The whole family can come forward at Communion time. Parents and family members who are not able to receive Communion can still come forward and receive a blessing. They are examples of faith to their children.

Pray Always

→ ## PART OF THE MASS: *Prayer after Communion*

Catechist notes

The Prayer after Communion is different for each Sunday Mass. We ask God's help to follow in the footsteps of Jesus and help people in need. The *Catechism of the Catholic Church* reminds us "The Eucharist commits us to the poor" (1397). We are one in Jesus Christ.

Sharing question

What would the world be like if everyone lived what Jesus Christ taught us?

Exploring the Mass

Jesus showed us how we are capable of living. We are to be people of compassion and mercy. God sends us to help others. Each of us has gifts and talents that we can share with others. If every person lived as Jesus taught us, what a wonderful world this would be.

After we have offered our own prayers to God, the priest prays the Prayer after Communion in the name of all of us. We stand for this prayer and when the presider says, "Through Christ our Lord," we respond "Amen." We know that all things are possible through Christ.

Learning activity

Use prayer prompts

The Eucharist unites us with God and one another. We are to be people of prayer in all things at Mass and outside of Mass too. Prayer prompts help children learn to pray in their own words. Ask children to choose a prayer prompt and write a short prayer to God.

Prayer prompts

- Thank God for being with you in all times and places of your life.
- Ask God to help you live in peace with others.
- Pray for people who are struggling to get through each day.
- Pray to trust in God even when times are difficult.
- Ask the Holy Spirit to help you make good choices.

Children's take-home idea

God has a purpose for your life that only you can fulfill. Ask God this week to help you become all that God created you to be. We are called to share our God-given talents and abilities with others.

Praying together

God of Glory,
fill our hearts with hope in you,
and fill our lives with love for others.
May we be people of prayer
in everything we do each day.
Help us witness to the power
of your love now and always.
Amen.

PART OF THE MASS:
Prayer after Communion

FAMILY IDEAS

The prayer after Communion is different for each Mass. We give thanks to God and ask God's help to go out and follow in the footsteps of Jesus. The *Catechism of the Catholic Church* reminds us "The Eucharist commits us to the poor" (1397). We are called to care about other people, to work for justice, and to make the world a better place.

▷ Stress to children that we are to think of how we can help others rather than what we want other people to do for us. For many children this requires a different way of thinking. Start small by asking children to make cards for someone who is sick.

▷ Teach very young children to pray using an echo prayer. Say one short phrase at a time, and let the children echo the words. Here is a sample. *Dear God* (echo), *thank you for making the world* (echo) *and for making me* (echo). *Help me to love others* (echo). *Amen* (echo).

FAMILY PRAYER

God of Glory, give us hearts full of hope, and lives filled with love for others. Show us how to live as a family with love and compassion toward others. May we witness to your love and share the good news of Jesus Christ with others. Amen.

Note to First Communion families

After we say own prayers to God, we pray together as the priest reads the prayer after Communion. We respond "Amen" as we make the prayer our own. Praying together reminds us that receiving Jesus Christ in the Eucharist is done as part of a community. Our relationship with God involves other people.

Live Like Jesus

⮕ PART OF THE MASS: *Concluding Rites*

Catechist notes

Through the Eucharist we are united with God and with one another. We are to be Eucharistic people who live the greatest commandment—to love God and love others—until we come together again to celebrate at Mass.

Sharing question

How can we serve others as Jesus showed us?

Exploring the Mass

As disciples of Jesus Christ, we are to share God's love with others. God sends us to help others. We were created to live as a community of God's people. We must support and encourage one another.

The concluding rite has three main parts:

- Blessing
- Sending forth
- Closing song

Through our prayers and our actions, we give thanks to our God, who created us, loves us, and walks with us through the coming week. Hopefully, what we do at Mass on Sunday will continue in our lives during the week ahead.

Learning activity

Make kindness cards

Encourage children to share God's love by being people of kindness. Write "Kindness Card" with a red marker at the top of white index cards or print off six per page on white card stock and then cut apart. Ask children to think of ways to share kindness with others. For example:

- read a story to a younger child;
- talk to a child at school who seems sad;
- invite a new neighbor child to play at your house;
- make a get-well card for a person who is sick;
- visit an elderly neighbor with your family;
- donate new coloring books and crayons to a children's hospital.

Each child writes on the card one act of kindness that they will do during the coming week. They take home the card as a reminder. In this way, children put into action what they learn.

Children's take-home idea

Look for ways to serve others this week as Jesus did. Help someone who is sick, sad, worried, lonely, or in need of a friend. If everyone did this, the world would be a better place. Share the light of Christ with other people.

Praying together

Jesus, Teacher and Redeemer,
you are the light of our world
and the light of our lives.
Help us to be people of compassion
who witness to your love
by the way we live each day.
Amen.

PART OF THE MASS:
Concluding Rites

FAMILY IDEAS

Renewed and strengthened by our time together at Mass, we go out to live as Jesus Christ showed us. The word **Mass** comes from a Latin word meaning "sending." We are sent from Mass to announce the good news of Jesus Christ. Our words, our actions, and our example of faith show people who Jesus Christ is in our lives.

▶ As the primary teachers of your children in the ways of faith, you teach them about God's love in the ordinary moments of daily life. When you tenderly tuck them in at night, when you listen to what they say, and when you care for them, you show God's love to your children.

▶ Continue to spend time together after Sunday Mass. Go for a walk, play a game together, look at family pictures, or call or Skype other family members. In this way we make Sundays special family days.

FAMILY PRAYER

Jesus, Teacher and Redeemer, you are the light of the world and the light of our lives. Help our family to walk always in the light and show your light to others. May we be people of compassion who witness to your love by the way we live each day. Amen.

Note to First Communion families

Teach empathy to your First Communion child by asking questions such as: How would you feel if there were no doctors to go to if you were sick? What would it be like if you were hungry and there was no food to eat? How do you think children feel who live in a refugee camp? This helps children become more aware of the feelings of others.

God Blesses Our Lives

→ ## PART OF MASS: *Blessing*

Catechist notes

Before we are sent out to share the good news of Jesus Christ, the priest asks God to bless us. Blessings have always been a part of the Mass and a part of the church. The blessing at Mass is for all of us who have gathered together.

Sharing question

In whose name does the priest bless us at the end of Mass?

Exploring the Mass

The priest offers us a blessing in God's name, Father, Son, and Holy Spirit. We respond, "Amen." We ask God's help for what we will do during the coming week. With the blessing of God, we go forth to live as Jesus taught us and to share the good news with others.

We can ask God's blessing at home too. God is with us always and hears our prayers. We can ask God's blessing to begin each day, or when we face challenges, or for another person.

Learning activity

Participate in a gesture prayer

With a gesture prayer, children can pray for God's blessing in their lives. The learners say the words and do the gestures line by line, following the catechist. This helps children pray with their whole selves.

Lord Jesus Christ,	*make sign of cross*
thank you for coming to us	*hands over heart*
as Teacher and Savior.	*point to palms*

You showed us by your words	*hands by mouth*
and by your actions	*nod head*
that we are to love all people	*arms stretched*
in your holy name.	*point to palms*
We ask your blessing on us	*hands on heart*
so that we may share your love	*arms outstretched*
through what we say	*hands by mouth*
and what we do each day.	*nod head*
Amen.	*fold hands*

Children's take-home idea

Praise God for your blessings this week. Think about how you can share those blessings with someone else. In this way you can be a blessing in the life of another person. With God, all things are possible.

Praying together

God of blessings,
we thank you for all the blessings
that you have given us.
We thank you for the beauty of creation
and the people who care about us.
We thank you most of all
for your love for each one of us.
Help us to see your blessings
in our world and in our lives.
Amen.

PART OF MASS:
Blessing

FAMILY IDEAS

The celebrant of the Mass asks God to bless us as we are sent forth to share the good news of Jesus Christ. With God's help we go forth to live what we believe. We can then bless the lives of others by our words and actions.

▷ God is with us always, and we can ask God to bless us and our lives during the week. We can also pray for God's blessing on other people too, especially as they face challenges in their lives. In this way we remember that all our blessings come from our God.

▷ Bless your child before he or she goes to sleep at night. Make the sign of the cross on their forehead with your thumb. Say, "May God bless you, Father, Son, and Holy Spirit." This helps children remember that God cares about us.

FAMILY PRAYER

God of blessings, we thank you for all the blessings that you have given our family. Thank you especially for the gift of one another and the love we share as a family. Open our hearts to your blessings in our world and in our lives. Amen.

Note to First Communion families

Blessings are important. Families can ask God's blessing on the child who is preparing for First Communion. This can be done after saying grace before meals or any time your family gathers for prayer together. Continue to pray for your child after First Communion too.

Go and Share the Good News

➜ PART OF THE MASS: *Sending Forth*

Catechist notes

The word *Mass* comes from a Latin word meaning "sending." Renewed by the Eucharist, we are sent forth to live as disciples of Jesus Christ. We also share in the mission of the church to proclaim the good news of Jesus Christ to other people.

Sharing question

What are ways to share the good news of Jesus Christ?

Exploring the Mass

Our example of faith shows people who Jesus Christ is. The United States bishops remind us that "we must be missionary disciples, called to witness to Christ in every aspect of our lives" (*Living as Missionary Disciples*).

We are sent forth from Mass to share the gospel with others. Jesus came for all people. We show people who Jesus Christ is by our words and our actions. Some ideas are:

- invite people to Sunday Mass;
- show respect for people of all cultures;
- display a cross in your home as a sign of faith;
- tell someone who is sad about God's love;
- bring hope by serving others in need;
- pray to our God with other people.

Through the Mass, we celebrate who we are as God's people and all that God has done in our lives. We are renewed and strengthened by our time together and go out to live from Sunday to Sunday as Jesus Christ taught us to live.

Learning activity

Design a colorful heart

Provide patterns for the children so they can cut out large hearts from red card stock to remember God's love. This craft is fun for children to make. The children cut self-stick foam into squares in a variety of colors such as yellow, blue, orange, and green. They add the squares to make a colorful heart. Their colorful heart reminds them that we are called to share the good news of God's love with others.

Children's take-home idea

See how you can share God's love with someone this week. Maybe there is a new student in your school, a member of your family who is sick, or an elderly person at church. Open your heart and your life to others. Show them who Jesus Christ is by what you say and do.

Praying together

Jesus,
you are the light of the world
and the light of our lives.
Help us to walk always in the light
and show your light to others.
Strengthen us to live our faith
as we are sent forth from Mass
to share the good news of your love.
Amen.

PART OF THE MASS:
Sending Forth

FAMILY IDEAS

At the end of Mass, we are sent forth to live our faith. We share in the mission of the church to proclaim to others how much our God loves us and all that God has done for us. We are to live as Jesus taught us and see the face of Jesus in other people. There are many people in our world who need help in our communities and in our world.

▶ Brainstorm ideas that your family can do together to help others. This can include going as a family to meet a new neighbor, donating new craft supplies to a family shelter, or participating in a walk to benefit a children's charity.

▶ Create a kindness corner on your pantry door or other area. When a family member does something nice for someone else, let them put down what they did on a heart and put it on the door. Use heart sticky notes, if available. Watch the good deeds grow.

FAMILY PRAYER

Lord Jesus, help our family show compassion to others. May we witness to your love by the way we live each day. Help us reach out to people in need of a kind word or a helping hand. Guide us to live each day as your disciples. Amen.

Note to First Communion families

Plan a family service opportunity that involves your First Communion child. This can be making craft kits for a children's hospital or assembling welcome kits with personal care items for a shelter. Check family service ideas in your local community online.

Make a Difference

→ ## PART OF THE MASS: *Closing Song*

Catechist notes

Singing together is an important way to give praise to God. United in faith, we raise our hearts and voices to our Creator. We use the God-given gift of music to praise God and celebrate who God is in our lives.

Sharing question

How can we make a difference?

Exploring the Mass

We go out to witness to God's love for each person. We share God's love with others by our words, by our actions, and through our prayers. We can begin one person at a time. Encourage children and families to open their hearts to people who need a smile, a kind word, or a helping hand.

Play a song for the children that is sung as a closing song at Sunday Mass such as "Go Make a Difference" by Steve Angrisano and Tom Tomaszek. This lively song reminds children that we are the hands of Christ and we are called to make a difference. Encourage children to sing along while clapping to the beat.

Learning activity

Make a "hands for Jesus" cross

We leave Mass ready to become all that God has created us to be. We witness to God's love for all people. With the help of the Holy Spirit, we go out to continue the mission of Jesus Christ to the world.

Children can make individual crosses to remind them that we are to be the hands of Jesus Christ in our world. God sends us to help others. Give each child a craft foam cross. Provide labels that say "Hands for Jesus" to place in the center of each cross. Children will also need foam hand shape stickers in a variety of bright colors from a craft store or online. Children place the hand shapes on their individual crosses as a reminder that they are to help others in the name of Jesus Christ.

Children's take-home idea

Ask the Holy Spirit to guide you this week to follow in the footsteps of Jesus Christ. We are to share God's love with others by our words and actions. We can make a difference one person at a time.

Praying together

Holy Spirit, giver of life,
we thank you for all you have done
and continue to do in our lives.
Guide us to be the hands of Jesus
in our world today.
Fill our hearts and our lives
with faith in you, hope in our world,
and love for all people.
Amen.

PART OF THE MASS:
Closing Song

FAMILY IDEAS

We sing together the closing song at Mass. We praise God as we get ready to go out and live what we believe. We share God's love with others by our words, by our actions, and through our prayers. With the help of the Holy Spirit we can become all that God has created us to be.

➤ Start making a difference on the way out of Mass. Say, "Have a good day!" to someone who is leaving their pew as you are leaving yours, hold the door for someone, and have patience if the person ahead of you is elderly and walking slowly.

➤ What we celebrate at Mass, we continue to live in our lives during the week. Look for ways to praise God, live in peace, and serve others. In this way we make a difference one step and one person at a time. With God's help we go forth to live as we were created.

FAMILY PRAYER

Holy Spirit, Giver of life, we thank you for all you have done and continue to do in our lives. Guide us to be the hands of Jesus in our world today. Fill our family with faith in you and love for all people. Amen.

Note to First Communion families

Being Eucharistic people means reaching out to people living in poverty in our world. We are called to share the resources of our world. Become aware of the needs of others by looking at websites such as Catholic Relief Services. Talk about what you can do as a family to serve others in that name of Jesus Christ our Lord.

Ways to Encourage Families to Participate in Sunday Mass

Invite children to join the children's choir, become altar servers, or be involved in other ministries. Be sure families have details about these opportunities for their children, including the time and place of rehearsals or training.

Explore Sunday readings with a question each week. Discuss the question with the children and invite families to do this at home. It is wonderful if this question is in the Sunday bulletin too. This shows families how Scripture relates to their lives.

Ask children and families to participate in parish service projects, such as bringing food for the hungry to Mass. Explain the project and give families the details they need to make it easy for them to be involved.

Connect youth with other youth in the parish. Let youth and their families know about teen liturgies and group events such as bowling or serving a meal to people in need. Encourage youth to be a part of the parish community.

Welcome families with older children who have not yet prepared to receive the sacraments. Be understanding and let them know the first step they should take. Connect them with the people and information they need.

Promote use of the parish website, Facebook page, and other social media where busy families can find information twenty-four hours a day. In this way they can more easily connect with their parish activities and feel more a part of the parish.

Explain children's liturgy of the word if your parish offers it. Let them know that the children go to another area to explore the readings during the Mass and then return to their families. Be sure that families understand that their children are invited to be a part of this.

Be sure to welcome families with special needs children at Mass. See what your parish can offer for these families, such as special picture missals or sign interpretations. Let the families know how their children can be included in sacramental preparation.

Share information about the parish patron saint and celebrations of the feast day. This helps families know what is going on in the parish. Encourage participation in the feast day Mass and celebration. Give out holy cards of the patron saint.

Provide family-friendly ideas to families with young children. Give families information about where they can get children's Bibles and prayer books. Provide website addresses with ideas for families in the bulletin.

Encourage families to pray together at Sunday Mass and at home. Give them prayers and ideas during each liturgical season to help them tie in the liturgy with their lives. Give out copies of materials so families don't have to search for ideas.